UNVEILING HEARTS

A COLLECTION OF POETRY

BY

SURYANSHU

CLEVER FOX PUBLISHING
Chennai, India

Published by CLEVER FOX PUBLISHING 2023
Copyright © Suryanshu 2023

Chapter 1:
Seeds of Friendship

Poems that celebrate the beginning of a deep friendship, capturing the bond, trust, and shared experiences.

A Priceless Bond

In a realm of fortunes,
I found a gem,
A friend like you,
a priceless emblem.
Lucky I am
to have you by my side,
A caring soul,
in whom I confide.

You've shown kindness and love,
without a doubt,
Always there for me,
without a second thought.
Adapting and adjusting,
through thick and thin,
Your unwavering support,
a cherished win.

Who says bonds require
endless time to bloom?
When hearts are genuine,
connections find room.
In an instant,
I knew you were true.
A friend I could count on,
through and through.

Empathy, care, and sweetness
define your soul,
A beacon of light,
making my world whole.
Stay as you are,
my dear friend so dear,
May eternal happiness
be always near.

May your spirit remain
strong and bright,
Guiding you through
both joy and plight.
Together, we'll face
life's tests and trials,
Bound by a friendship
that forever smiles.

Flavors of Friendship

Spicy chats and bitter truths,
Sweet memories and carefree youth,
All the flavors of life we blend,
And you became my flavorous best friend.

From hot debates to cool retreats,
We weathered storms and conquered feats,
With every challenge, we learned and grew,
And our bond strengthened, solid and true.

Through laughter, tears,
and everything in between,
Our friendship stood strong,
A rare and precious scene,
For in a world so fleeting and fleeting,
Our connection was steadfast,
never retreating.

So here's to the spicy chats
and bitter truths,
The sweet memories that made us swoon,
And to the flavorous of friendships,
oh so rare,
That brings joy and love beyond compare.

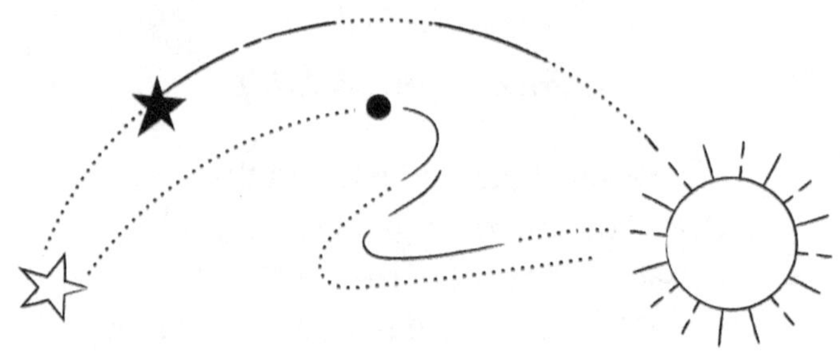

Celestial Souls

In the realm of falling,
I'll be your steady ground,
no depths too deep,
no challenges profound.
No vibes of loneliness
shall linger by your side,
for I'll be your companion,
matching stride for stride.

The ache that burdens,
we'll gently ease,
together we'll conquer,
finding inner peace.
No cherished moments
shall slip through our embrace,
as we build a bond,
that time can not replace.

In our friendship's sanctuary,
no grudges shall reside,
understanding and forgiveness
forever coincide.
know, my dear,
how cherished you truly are,
a celestial soul, a guiding star.

Chapter 2:
Blossoming Love

Poems that explore the transition from friendship to romantic feelings, portraying the excitement and complexity of this shift.

Shifting Tides

In friendship's realm,
we laughed and we played,
bound by moments cherished,
memories made.
But as time flowed by,
a shift took hold,
emotions awakened,
stories yet untold.

Eyes met with a spark,
hearts skipped a beat,
unveiling a path uncharted,
bittersweet.
From shared laughter
to lingering glances,
a dance of feelings,
newfound romances.

Yet with this shift,
complexities arise,
fear and uncertainty,
in our love's disguise.
Can friendship endure
the romantic tide?
A delicate balance,
where emotions collide.

Navigating the currents,
we take the leap,
unveiling a love
that runs soul-deep.
Exploring the depths
of what might be,
With hearts entwined,
setting each other free.

In this journey,
emotions intertwine,
friendship's foundation,
now love's lifeline.
Excitement and complexity
walk hand in hand,
as we embark on
love's intricate, beautiful strand.

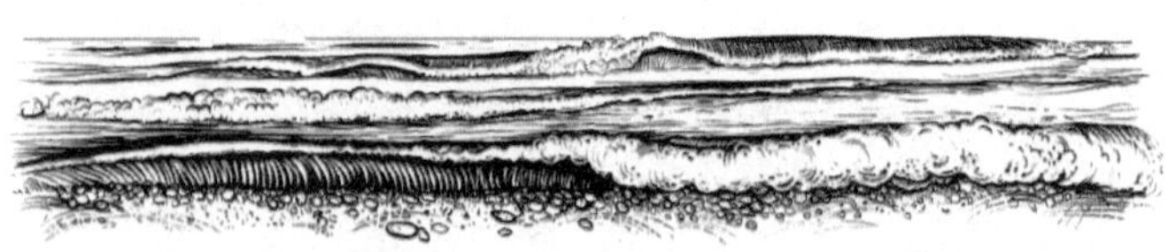

Tides of Passion

In the ocean of love,
the currents sway,
the emotions dance,
in a mysterious way.
With every dive,
euphoria may be found,
yet beneath the surface,
dangers can abound.

In the depths of affection,
hearts may soar,
an ethereal realm,
where dreams explore.
But amidst the waves,
caution must be taken,
for love's depths can
leave the soul forsaken.

The waters may sparkle
with passion's gleam,
Yet beneath the surface,
turmoil may teem.
Navigating the tides
of desire and despair,
one must tread carefully,
with love's burden to bear.

So swim with caution,
with eyes open wide.
Feel the currents,
let your heart be your guide.
Embrace the joy,
but be mindful of the deep.
In the ocean of love,
both diving and drowning may creep.

Symphony of Love

In love's warm embrace,
solace found anew.
On cloud nine,
my heart's rhythm beats for you.
Each moment shared,
a vibrant tapestry,
a symphony of colors,
a dazzling reverie.

Your presence,
a sweet melody that softly lingers,
enchanting my senses,
dispelling worries and fears.
Excitement surges,
a joyous dance in my core,
as we wander together
on love's captivating shore.

Whispers of nervousness
tremble on my lips,
words falter and stumble,
like unsteady ships.
Butterflies flutter,
painting our love's gentle start,
a dance of emotions,
an eternal work of art.

With each touch,
a spark ignites,
a fervent fire,
In this love's waltz,
I never tire.
You, my love,
the masterpiece I adore,
In your embrace,
I crave forevermore.

I surrender,
intoxicated by this sweet elation,
love guiding me
without a hint of hesitation.
In your love,
my true delight takes flight,
a kaleidoscope of emotions,
forever alight.

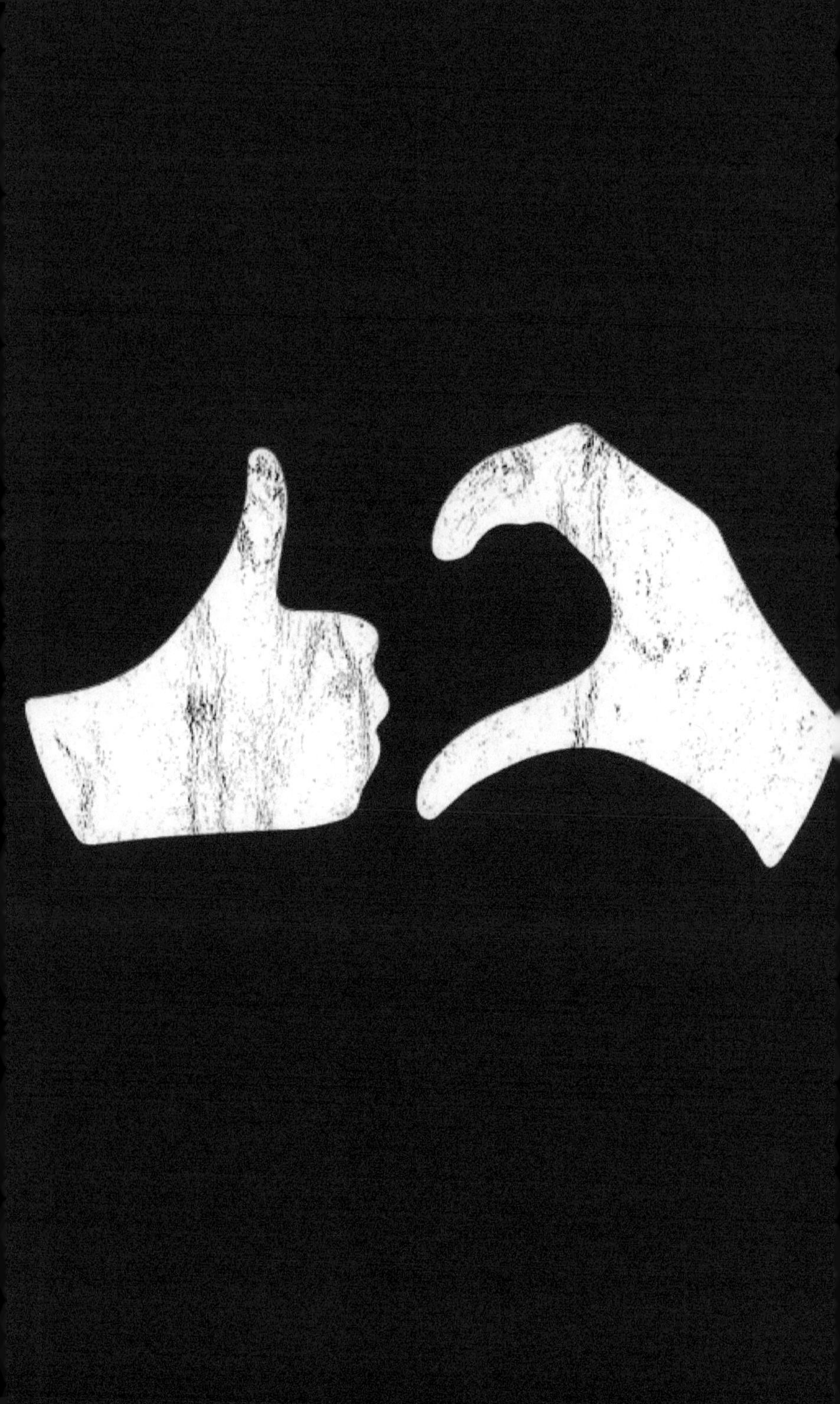

Chapter 3:
The Friendzone

Poems that delve into the bittersweet realm of unrequited love or being in the friendzone, conveying the longing, frustration, and emotional turmoil.

Illusions of Permanence

In the shadow of absence,
they turned to you,
seeking solace,
as their favorite withdrew.
They painted a picture of permanence,
so grand,
But you were just a temporary option,
at their command.

They made you believe
in a love that would endure,
A bond so strong,
of that you were sure.
Yet behind closed doors,
their heart did stray,
leaving you as a convenient choice,
day by day.

But now you see through
the veil of their disguise,
no longer blinded by
false promises and lies.
You deserve more than
being an easy substitute,
A love that's genuine,
not one to refute.

So rise above their
shallow intentions and game,
embrace your worth
and refuse to be tamed.
You are not a temporary
option to be found,
But a treasure deserving
of love that's profound.

Sowing Hope

Far from my homeland,
I sowed my favorite crop,
pouring into it my time,
money, and countless sweat drops.

The climate proved a challenging foe,
yet hope within me continued to grow.
When asked if I had sown, I'd often deny,
to avoid sounding foolish,
I'd let the question fly.

Advice came pouring from those around,
and I listened, my ears eager to resound.
Though doubts loomed, my heart held on,
to the dream of my favorite crop,
not yet gone.

The land, for now, lies barren and still,
but I gather ideas,
seeking inspiration's thrill,
I play on its soil, a respite from the grind,
while awaiting the day my dreams unwind.

Teddy Bear

To have me in your life,
You paid a hefty price.
Maybe this is the reason,
I am still there.
See how similar I am to a teddy bear.

You come to me when you are alone,
We play together, have fun,
I am always there.
See how similar I am to a teddy bear.

One fortunate day, as luck finds its way,
What if you find a better teddy bear?
Happy for you, but afraid I am,
What if you leave me somewhere?

Even if you do so,
I will always care.
But I will become quiet,
Just like a teddy bear.

The Home of Hope

The home of hope can not be shared
for it has a single bed,
Either you abandon it or the loved one
but that's how you move ahead.

Invisible Strings

Those invisible strings that attach us,
they can not be seen,
but I can feel them every day.
I wish to be set free.

Chapter 4:
Fragile Bonds

Poems that examine the challenges, doubts, and vulnerabilities that arise when romantic feelings are present.

Good People, Bad Moments

Good people can also hurt,
though their intentions may be pure.
Caring people can sometimes neglect,
despite their love, they may forget.

Understanding people have their limits,
their patience may wane, their empathy may dim it.
Always there doesn't mean every time,
they may have their own battles to climb.

But these are not reasons to hate,
for every person has their own fate.
Rather, let's practice compassion and forgiveness,
and not judge others based on our own biases.

For life is a journey with many ups and downs,
and sometimes, good people may wear a frown.
Let's be there for each other, through thick and thin,
and strive to be better, and let love always win.

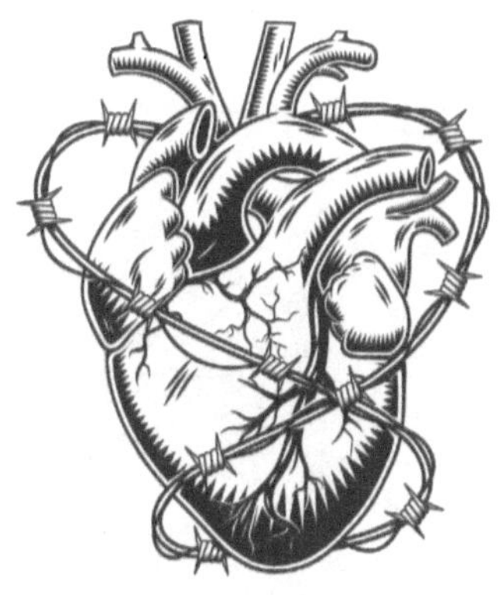

Bonds and Boundaries

It's alright to give of yourself,
but not your physical shell,
to honor boundaries,
ensuring your limits won't quell.
Let go of demands,
yet hold some expectations dear,
lower your walls,
while respecting yourself clear.

Prioritize their needs,
while cherishing other bonds,
If reciprocity fades,
It's okay to reflect and respond.
It's okay, as long as
we don't cause harm,
finding solace,
knowing we gave our charm.

Boundless Love, Measured Giving

Let your love be boundless, free,
a shining beacon for all to see.
But let it not consume your life,
and cause you pain, turmoil and strife.

Limit it to those who cherish you,
and whose hearts you hold close and true.
For they are the ones who matter most,
and whose love sustains
and keeps you close.

Let your love be pure and bright,
a guiding star in the darkest night,
But do not let it take control,
and drain your spirit, heart and soul.

So let your love be confined to few,
but let it fill your life anew.
For with a heart that's strong and true,
you'll find your way, no matter what you do.

Paths of Intent

What they could do,
a realm of possibility,
Yet what they would do,
holds true authenticity.
Potential and intention
may intertwine,
But actions reveal
the path they align.

Confusion arises when
lines become blurred,
Expectations misled,
assumptions incurred.
For what they could do
shouldn't be confused,
With what they would do,
where truths are fused.

In the depths of intent,
motivations reside,
Choices and desires,
the compass to guide.
So look beyond could
and focus on would,
To understand the essence,
intentions that stood.

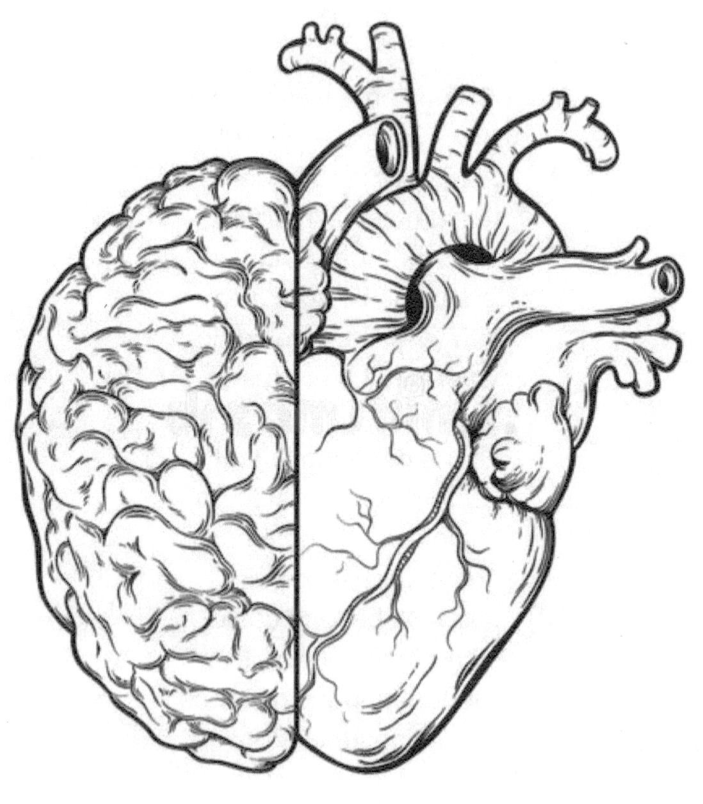

Heart vs Mind

Closeness bears
a cost on tender emotions,
a toll the heart can't always
withstand potions.
Yet the mind fails to
grasp this tender plea,
yearning for connection,
overlooking the fee.

In the pursuit of connection,
hearts may bleed,
drained by the depth
of the bond they heed.
But the mind,
driven by logic and demand,
neglects the heart's plea,
unable to understand.

For the heart can't afford
the price of every bond,
Its fragility at stake,
easily abscond.
Yet the mind, relentless
in its quest for nearness,
battles the heart,
driven by its own fierceness.

In the interplay of
heart and mind,
a balance that we ache for
may we find.
May understanding dawn,
a harmonious blend,
where emotions are honored,
and closeness transcends.

Chapter 5:
Melancholic Reflections

Poems that reflect on heartbreak, loss, and the aftermath of navigating the complexities of love and friendship.

Memory Lane (His Perspective)

I want to stroll down on our memory lane,
Would you join me for a walk?
This silence between us is killing me,
Do you also wish to talk?

I have so many good things piled up,
Would you like me to share?
If I said I still love you,
Will you let me show how much I care?

Memory Lane (Her Perspective)

I can hear the pain in your voice,
the hurt that you try to hide.
But going back to the past,
is something I cannot decide.

We had our moments, our memories,
but they belong to a time gone by.
And though it hurts me too,
we cannot keep living a lie.

I hope you find the closure you seek,
and can find peace within your heart.
But for us to move forward,
we need to stay apart.

So take care of yourself,
and let us both move on.
For the future holds so much,
and the past is already gone.

Lost in Autumn

Let me scroll through our memories,
let me find a reason.
or does autumn come in bonds too,
and it's the fall season.

Let me check with myself,
if I didn't make the right effort.
or am I not comfortable anymore,
and all I do is always hurt?

Maybe we got too comfortable,
and took each other for granted;
or perhaps we lost our way,
and our paths became slanted.

I thought we were evergreen,
we might not have to shed.
What once seemed so healthy,
how can it be dead?

I wish we could have held on,
to the love we once shared.
But sometimes, things just change,
and the bond becomes impaired.

Now it's time to let go,
and embrace the season of change.
To cherish what we had,
and not see it as strange.

Sailing on a Dried Ocean

On a dried ocean, we sailed.
still fearing we would sink,
not realizing that
long ago, we failed.
Going to savor our doom once again,
on a dried ocean, we sailed.

All the beautiful water bodies,
we chose to reject,
for they weren't the ones,
we fantasized about.
Such a pity for our obstinacy,
we chose a dried ocean to sail.

We craved for someone to help,
yet chose to stay silent.
It was obvious, but sadly not visible,
that on a dried ocean one can not sail.

Memories: The Two-Edged Sword

It's funny how the good memories,
can sometimes hurt the most.
The ones we thought were carefree,
now leave us feeling lost.

The flashbacks of our happy days,
once brought us so much joy.
But now they leave us in a daze,
and feelings we can't avoid.

It's not that the bad memories don't sting,
but somehow they seem to fade.
Perhaps it's because they don't bring,
the same intense emotions we've made.

So when the good memories start to hurt,
and the pain feels hard to bear,
remember that they also give us worth,
and moments to cherish
that we should share.

Wildfire

In the farms of my sorrows,
I shall have to cause a wildfire.
For I can't bury them deep,
as the soil of the heart doesn't reap
joyous fruits on the seeds of sorrow.

Chapter 6:
Inner Healing

Poems that focus on self-discovery, healing, and finding strength after experiencing the challenges of love and friendship.

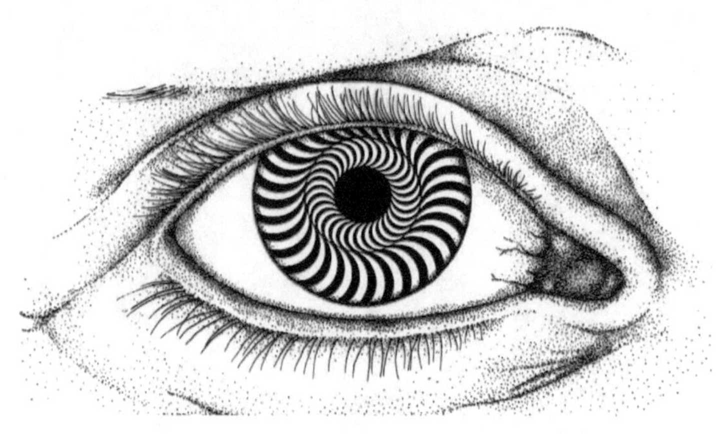

Different Perspectives

In the grand tapestry
of existence, we find,
countless stories
interwoven, intertwined.
Each person, a chapter,
resplendent and true,
with tales that unfold,
revealing a different view.

To some, they're an opus,
a masterpiece complete,
rich narratives, vibrant hues,
emotions replete.
Their pasts and aspirations,
like ink on the page,
a symphony of dreams,
a boundless stage.

Yet, in their eyes,
we may be just a trace,
a fleeting imprint,
a barely noticed embrace.
A footnote in their records,
small and slight,
a memory that may fade,
like whispers in the night.

Not that we're insignificant,
cast aside,
but perspectives diverge,
worlds collide.
We all possess lenses,
through which we gaze,
different values cherished,
and diverse pathways.

So, let's not dwell on
slights or harbor disdain.
Let understanding and
appreciation remain.
Embrace the diversity
that sets us apart,
a testament to the beauty
of a unified heart.

In this vast realm,
we're all one of a kind,
A treasure trove of tales,
waiting to unwind.
Though our journeys may diverge,
not the same,
We can honor each other's light
without blame.

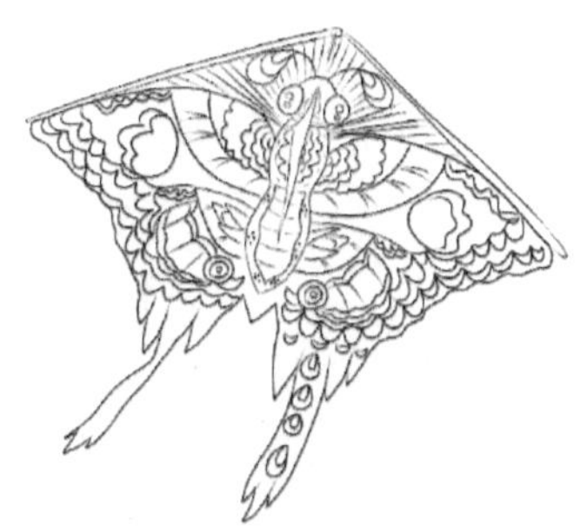

The Kite's Tale

Tied in a knot, held by their grip,
do you believe you're soaring free?
Your movements dictated by their whim,
you pretend to be content,
but are you truly?

Is it the world you're deceiving,
or is it yourself you're lying to?
Pretending you're all settled and believing,
that you're truly happy, when it's not true.

It's time to break free of the ties that bind,
and take control of your own fate.
The world may try to keep you confined,
but your spirit is too strong to be contained.

So spread your wings and take flight,
embrace your true self and soar high.
No longer controlled by others' might,
you'll discover the freedom
to live and thrive.

Howl of the Inner Demons

Oh hushed voices within,
cease thy piercing screams.
Dwell instead in the shadows,
and let my slumber be serene.

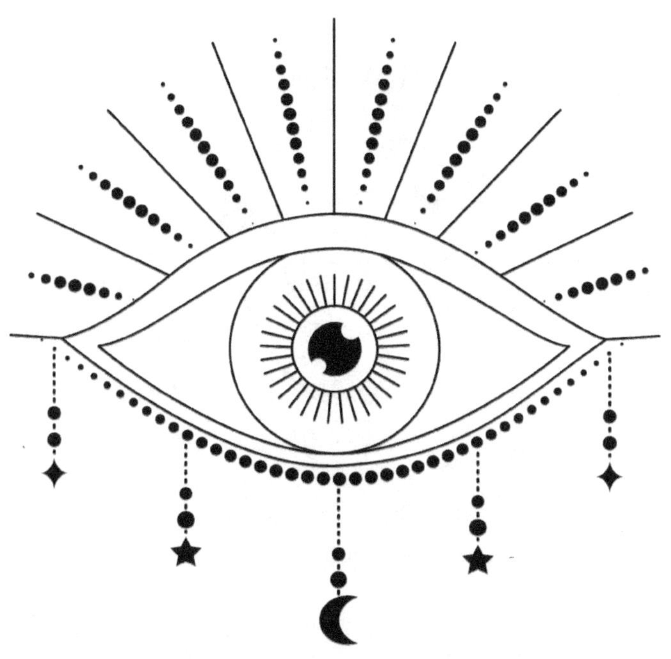

Beyond Sight

Sometimes we need to
remember that,
though eyes
bring us all beauty,
peace comes in only
when they are closed.

The Library of Memories

Within the vast library of
my memories, I roam,
One section beckons me,
the familiar tome,
I find solace in
revisiting stories of old,
Though new chapters await,
yet untold.

A strange pull
holds me in its grasp,
Resistance lingers,
an unyielding clasp,

The allure of the known,
the comfort it brings,
Why I resist the chance
to spread new wings.

Perhaps it's the fear of
losing cherished pages,
Neglecting the tales
that have weathered ages,
Or the uncertainty of
lending to others' hands,
Leaving voids in my collection,
like shifting sands.

In this vast expanse,
truths both known and unknown,
The weight of understanding,
the seeds yet unsown,
And the longing to unravel
the fragments unseen,
My heart hesitates,
uncertain of what it may mean.

Yet, amidst this dance of
longing and restraint,
I seek the balance,
where old and new acquaint,
For in the library of memories,
growth doesn't find its space,
Only by embracing the unfamiliar,
self-discovery takes place.

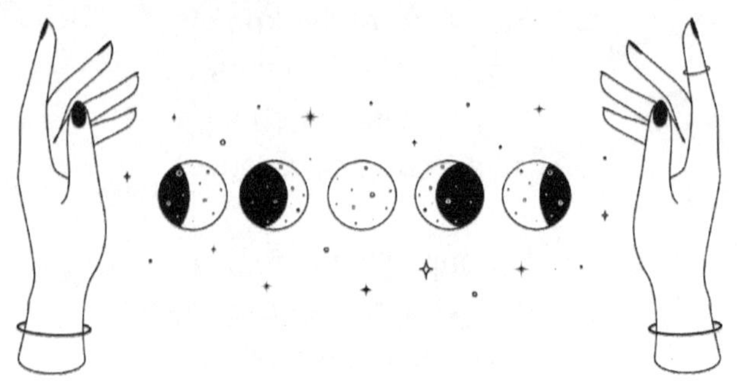

Eternal Phases

In the realm of dreams,
where emotions reside,
I wander through thoughts,
in a lunar tide.
To expect your radiance,
my dear moon, so bright,
Each passing day
would be a lofty sight.

For you, my muse,
possess a gentle grace,
A glow that soothes,
a calming embrace.
But even the moon
must concede and fade,
As the cycle turns,
it ventures in the shade.

Yet on the day
you choose to wane, depart,
Vanishing from sight,
a transient art,
May you find the strength
to face the night,
To conquer shadows,
your spirit ignites.

Let your light transcend,
inspire and heal,
Be a constant reminder
that hope is real.
Though the night may be long,
filled with despair,
Your resilience, dear moon,
will always be there.

Heartbreak and Healing

She faced her solitude
with an unmatched grace,
a heart that screamed
yet never lost its place.
Betrayed by those
she trusted the most,
she refused to become
a bitter host.

She didn't blame or shame
the ones who hurt her,
instead, she focused
on healing from within.
Though guilt weighed
heavy on her soul,
She didn't let
it take control.

She began to shed
the old skin she wore,
And emerged anew,
like never before.
Transformed into
someone unrecognizable,
She won over hearts,
so pure and undeniable.

Diamond Heart

You can't break me anymore,
you can't take my shine.
Until your love can afford me,
I choose to be only mine.

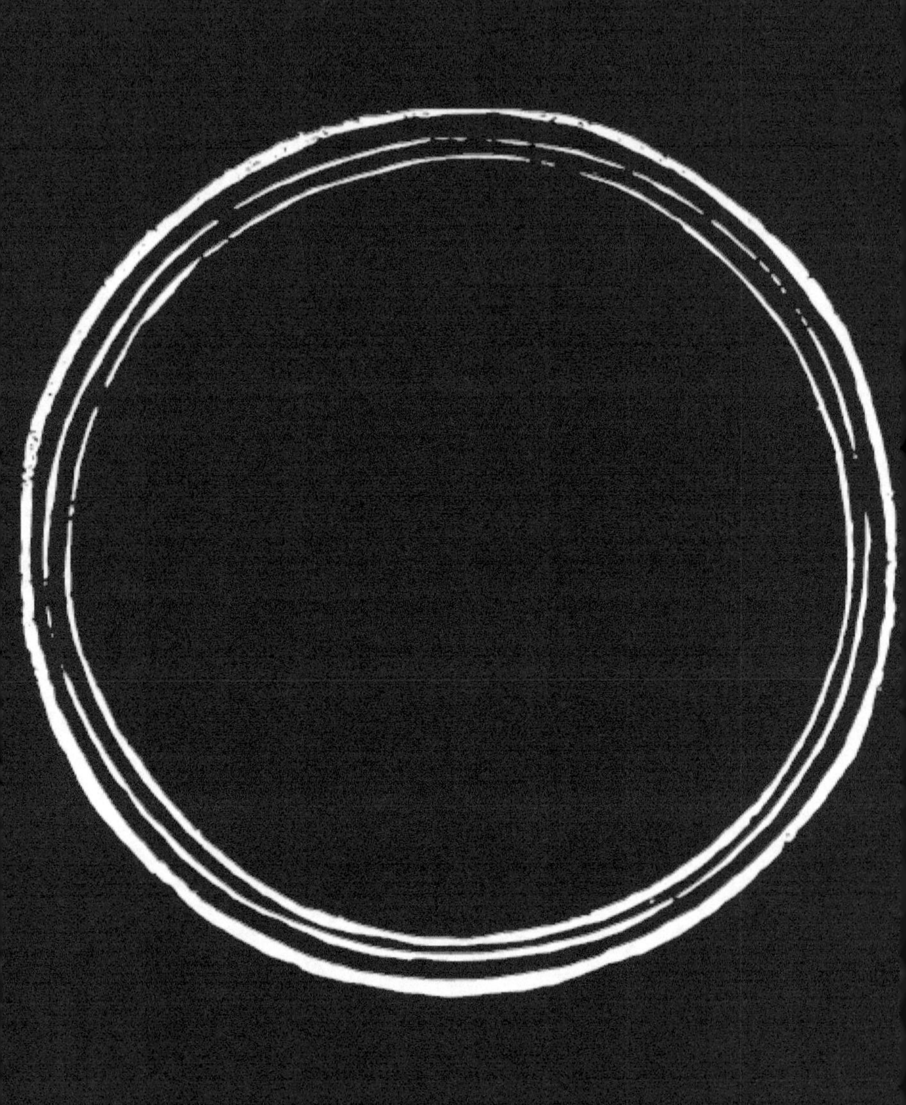

Chapter 7: Full Circle

Poems that revisit themes from the earlier chapters, showcasing the cyclical nature of love and friendship and the growth that comes with these experiences.

The Mosaic of Truth

Truth,
a mosaic woven with care,
an orchestra of shades,
intricate and rare.
From vibrant hues
to subtle blend,
each fragment holds
a tale to transcend.

In its kaleidoscope,
contradictions may appear,
layers of understanding,
both far and near.
For truths are multifaceted,
ever evolving,
unveiling depths,
mysteries dissolving.

Embrace the mosaic,
its intricate design,
in shades and colors,
revelations align.
For in the interplay of
light and shade,
truth's diverse essence is
beautifully displayed.

Seek not a single hue,
a singular decree,
but the mosaic's beauty,
where truths interweave.
In embracing their richness,
wisdom will bloom,
as we navigate life's
ever-shifting room.

The Vicious Cycle

Look fades in the light of care.
Care fades in the light of ignorance.
Ignorance fades in the light of apology.
Apology fades in the light of ego.
Ego fades in the light of looks.

Journeying Through the Unknown

Listen, o my sweet friend!
Someday, all things shall reach an end.
But until then, hold love dear,
Embrace each moment, let joy adhere.

Hold tight to life's wondrous flight,
Savor each moment, day and night.
With a heart that radiates delight,
Navigate through shadows, conquer your fights.

The future's tale remains untold,
Uncertain twists may unfold.
Yet amid the chaos and unknown strife,
Seek solace, find hope in the walks of life.

Hope for a future, radiant and bright,
Yet cherish the present, with all your might.
Let no dreams be lost in the fading light,
Live without boundaries, let your soul take flight.

Vintage Beauty

On the canvas of time,
they appear,
those vintage scars
that you hold dear.
An antique smile,
weathered with grace,
a passé demeanor,
a unique embrace.

Adorable they are,
in their originality,
unlike the ones
the modern claim as reality,
For in your essence,
a timeless flair,
you are a soul
untouched by trends and lair.

Those vintage scars
tell stories untold,
of battles fought,
and wisdom bold.
Each mark a testament
to strength and strife,
shaping the very
fabric of your life.

That antique smile,
a beacon bright,
radiates warmth,
igniting pure delight.
It whispers tales of
love and grace,
a lasting memory,
no time can erase.

The passé demeanor,
a touch refined,
a gentle nod
to a different kind,
In a world that rushes,
you stand apart,
a relic of grace,
a nostalgic art.

Embrace your uniqueness,
unswayed by time;
let your vintage scars
etch their rhyme.
For authenticity,
a rare find to hold;
you are a treasure beyond
what the modern mold.

Wings of Love

In my love for parrots,
a connection I find,
a kindred soul,
a bond intertwined.
Naughty, talkative,
smart, and fair,
your presence brings
joy I can not compare.

Oh, precious soul,
I love you so,
devoting myself to
make your world glow.
Preparing you for flight,
each and every day,
though time together
may slip away.

Destined for heights,
a purpose grand,
perhaps chosen by
god's guiding hand.
Setting you free,
your wings to explore,
yet providing care at
our verandah's door.

Food and water await,
a loving display,
even if you don't return,
I'll be okay.
For your growth,
I release you with pride,
knowing you'll thrive,
no need to hide.

Some may question,
your absence a worry,
but faith in our love,
I won't hurry.
With prayers and hope,
my heart will mend.
For love's devotion is steadfast,
my dear friend.

www.ingramcontent.com/pod-product-compliance
Lightning Source LLC
LaVergne TN
LVHW091210180726

843490LV00007B/2692